# CINDY AND CRISTABELLE'S

# BIG

## SCARE

## Book One of Lil' Steps Series

### WRITTEN BY LUCY SLOAN,
BA PSYCH, ACCP, CAATP, RPC

ACTIVITY BOOKLET BY
JOANNE LARIVIERE, RSW, MACP AND LUCY SLOAN

www.lilstepswellnessfarm.net

**It** was a hot summer day at Lil' Steps Farm and the animals were relaxing in the bright sun. The horses were standing in the green grass, the sheep were chewing on their cuds, and Wilbert the Pig and his big round belly happily rolled in the cool mud. They were all as relaxed as relaxed could be!

Wilbert the Pig loved to feel the cool breeze on his wet snout as he breathed in the fresh air. He would take deep piggy belly breaths—

### in and out, in and out, in and out.

His big round belly went up and down.

# "this is the life,"

he said with a content smile.

# Lil'

**Steps Farm was at** peace. Well, except for the fainting goats, Cindy and Cristabelle. Relaxing was not a thing that they did well . . . When Cindy and Cristabelle became scared or worried, they fainted!

4

As far as **Cindy** and Cristabelle were concerned, with all of the things that could go wrong on the farm, there was just so much to worry about! In fact, they were so good at worrying that they would worry all day and all night. They barely had time to do anything else at all.

Their minds raced with

# "what ifs."

"What if it's too sunny? We'll get sunburn and be sick!"

"What if it doesn't rain and then the grass does not grow? We'll have no food to eat!"

"What if there really is no food? then we'll be hungry! What will we do then?"

And then, every now and then, their

# BIGGEST

"what if" worry came round again . . .

"If the sun stops the rain and ALL the animals get hungry, what if the coyotes and bears and lions come?!"

7

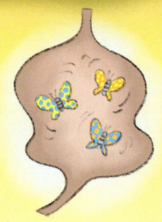

**At** this point in their worries Cindy and Cristabelle had scared themselves so much that they would feel it in their bodies. Cindy's tummy would start to ache and her neck would get very sore. She would be hit with a jolt of energy that made her feel like she needed to run. When Cristabelle became scared, she would stand as still as still could be. It felt like her body was frozen! She could feel her feet stuck to the ground.

Eventually, the two goats would start to feel hot and sweaty, their hearts would race, their chests would feel tight, and their legs would turn to jelly.

Then,

PLOP!

They would faint!

# At night their worries became the worst because their imaginations would grow and grow in the darkness. Their imaginations became as big as their worries and their worries became as big as their imaginations.

They would imagine the coyotes lurking in the forest with their big, big teeth and their little, mean black eyes. When they heard that Farmer Lucy had seen a coyote one time, their worries grew even bigger, and would not go away. In fact, the more they worried, the more the worries

grew, and grew, **and grew.**

**As** Wilbert rolled in the cool mud, all he could think about was how the mud felt so soothing on his big round belly. Wilbert snorted with joy,

## "Oink, oink, oink!"

He felt content as he took his slow, deep piggy belly breaths,

## in and out, in and out, in and out.

Wilbert enjoyed the simple things in life. He was a very happy pig.

But when Wilbert saw the goats worrying, he became concerned. "What are they worrying about? They should be enjoying this beautiful day! I should go and see what's wrong."

**Wilbert worked hard to** get his big round belly out of the mud, though it was so cool and delicious. His belly almost touched the ground as he walked toward the goats.

"Cindy and Cristabelle!

## Why do you look so worried?

With the bright sun, and the cool soft mud,
and the gentle breeze, why do you both look so upset?"

At the sound of an unexpected voice, Cindy jumped in fright, as high as high could be! Cristabelle had frozen in her tracks.

Then they became very angry.

"NEVER SNEAK UP ON US LIKE THAT!" Cindy yelled. "What if you were a coyote looking for lunch, or a lion ready to pounce, or a bear needing a snack?"

"But I am not," replied Wilbert, confused. "I am a pig. Not a coyote. Not a lion. Nor a bear."

15

**It** made Wilbert sad that the goats spent so much time worrying. He could not remember the last time they had played with him or any of the other farmyard animals. Then Wilbert had a great idea! He knew that the night would be full of stars and the moon would be full and bright.

"Why don't you come out to look for shooting stars with me tonight?" begged Wilbert with a smile.

# "Oh NO, NO, NO,

we could NEVER stay out at night! That's when all the scary things come out!" the goats replied. Wilbert smiled kindly at them and stated, "When you are ready, I would be happy to show you."

# that

night as their fears ran wild in their imaginations, they began to hear every little sound around them, as if the sounds were as loud as loud could be.

Then they heard the

# SNAP! CRUNCH!

of branches.

Cindy panicked,

# "I knew it!

There must be something in the bush!

It must be a bear!"

18

"Or a coyote with big big **BIG** teeth and beady black eyes!" replied Cristabelle.

"Or a hungry lion ready to pounce!" they agreed.

# the

noise became louder and louder and

# LOUDER

as the goats stood frozen in fear. A scary shadow moved across the light shining from the barn. Two big eyes peeked out from the dark forest.

Closer and closer the shadow crept, as slow as slow could be. And bigger and bigger the shadow became, as big as big could be. And louder and louder the footprints became!

## As loud as loud could be!

**Cindy wanted to scream.** Cristabelle wanted to hide. But they were STUCK as stuck as stuck could be. The goats were just feeling like they were going to faint, when, all of a sudden,

out of the dark forest,

jumped a

# HUGE,
# SCARY,
# HUNGRY . . .

# rabbit!

# Wait—a rabbit?!

The goats blinked in surprise. In front of them
stood a cute little rabbit. He looked at them and
waved, and then continued hopping around happily.

# PHEW!

The goats both fell to the ground, exhausted from their big scare.

"At least we are safe this time," said Cindy.

"Yes, for now we can sleep and stop all of this worrying!"

## And yet the worries continued to

# grow . . .

# the

**next day, as sleepy** as sleepy could be, the goats dragged themselves out of their soft straw bed. They looked at each other with sadness in their eyes. They felt as sad as sad could be.

"We got so scared and couldn't sleep from worrying, when nothing bad actually happened," Cindy muttered sorrowfully.

"Yes, and we missed out on having fun with Wilbert," mumbled Cristabelle.

The goats knew what they had to do.
They would learn to be more like Wilbert the Pig!

29

# they
## found Wilbert lying happily

in his cool mud bath, grunting with pleasure.

"Wilbert, we need your help!" cried the goats. "Can you teach us how to let go of our worries?" A big grin spread across Wilbert's face! He was so happy the goats had asked for his help. And he knew just what to do.

# All

day long, Wilbert showed the goats
how to relax and have fun. The goats
learned how to roll in the cool mud while
breathing deep piggy belly breaths,

## in and out, in and out, in and out.

They wagged their tails as they ate his
delicious slop and paid attention to the
feel of the sun warming their bodies. Then
they hopped and skipped and jumped around
in their healthy, happy bodies!

# After

**a few days of** playing with Wilbert and the farm animals, eating yummy slop, and sleeping soundly in their soft beds at night, they felt so happy and safe. They realized that when they paid attention to the good things in life, like Wilbert did, they were able to be happy without their heads being full of worry. And when they did begin to worry, Wilbert reminded them to take deep piggy belly breaths, just like him. When they did, they felt much more relaxed.

It took practice, but once the goats began to live outside of their scared imaginations, like Wilbert, they began to see the world differently . . .

The leaves were greener on the trees.

The sun felt good on their coats and gave them energy.

Even their food tasted better!

in and out, in and out, in and out.

in and out, in and out, in and out.

Today, in the soft and cool mud,
the goats and the pig all lay, bathing.

# "This is the life,"

they all agreed,
sighing happily and breathing
deep piggy belly breaths.

# The End

# LIL' STEPS WELLNESS FARM

# ACTIVITY BOOKLET

CO-AUTHORED BY LUCY SLOAN,
BA PSYCH, ACCP, CAATP, RPC
AND
JOANNE LARIVIERE, RSW, MACP

Introduction to Worry and Fear:
A Child-Centred Approach to Effectively Managing
Childhood Worries

# Activity Booklet

**H**ere at the farm there is a mantra that we follow and teach: A problem is only a problem if it causes a problem.

If worry and fear cause distress in your child's day-to-day life, then you have a problem that needs to be addressed.

As a Certified Animal Therapy Professional, I have been extremely lucky to help children address difficulties with anxiety with the assistance of my animal co-workers. The animals at Lil' Steps Farm each have their own unique stories, personalities, and life experiences. They provide acceptance, understanding, and learning opportunities to children struggling with a variety of difficulties.

The story in this book is based on true events and characters here at the farm. The hope is that with this story and the others in the series, children will be able to identify with the characters and gain a better understanding of what worry and fear are, how they are experienced, and most importantly, how to manage them effectively. While this booklet is primarily for the parents and/or guardians, there are Lil' Learning Lessons, identified throughout, that you can share and reflect on, either while reading the book with your child or after reading.

# Activity Booklet table of Contents

# Chapter 1

## Fundamentals for Parents, Caregivers, and Teachers

Did you know that 100% of children have worries? And guess what? That's okay! Fear is a normal human emotion that lets us know if and when we may be in danger. We *need* worry and fear to function and stay safe.

There are times, however, that the worry instinct kicks in when no real danger is present. This manifests in irrational fear, as is the case for Cindy and Cristabelle, who are continually worrying about coyotes, bears, and lions appearing with no evidence to suggest that they will. Initially, their fear may have begun from the one time a coyote had come close to the farm. Though it has never happened since, the fright that the danger caused has stayed with them, informing how they now see the world.

The same can be true for many children; they may hear of a story of a house being struck by lightning and be so frightened by that possibility that the fear becomes bigger and they begin to fear every single storm. Their rational fear, of fire, for instance, becomes irrational, yet very real to them. This is where difficulties arise. In the goats' case, this fear became irrational when their worry grew from a coyote's visit to include bears and lions; in reality there are no lions near the farm to fear in the first place.

Throughout the years at Lil' Steps Farm, the combination of worry-and-fear has been one of the most prevalent difficulties that parents and caregivers come to us seeking help for. For some children, its degree can meet the requirements of a medical diagnosis, such as an anxiety disorder. For so many other children such worries fall within the normal range, though they can become problematic with little to no warning.

Common childhood worries include (but are not limited to): separation anxiety from caregivers ("Please don't leave me!"); school-based worries (friends, academics, new routines, transitions); reassurance seeking ("Please tell me it will be okay."); night-time worries (bad guys, the dark, noises); and weather worries (tornadoes, storms, strong winds, hail). The activities in this booklet will help your child overcome these worries and fears by guiding them to become more aware of where, why, and how their worries affect them.

# Activity Booklet

We strongly believe that as "helper adults" we are a key component to teaching and supporting children in this process. As such, this booklet is an interactive, fun, and child-friendly tool for teaching children that they can be worried and afraid without being pathologically so. Some chapters are tailored to you, the helper adult(s), and others to both you and your child. With this book and your help, your child will learn to understand his or her worries, take charge of them, and create a worry toolbox to help manage worry and fear along the way!

A note on reassurance seeking: Children often look to trusting adults in their lives to provide them with reassurance that nothing bad will happen and that their worries won't come true. Although reassurance does work in the short term, it actually negatively reinforces the worry in the long term. As adults we often try to *fix* the fear or worry in our children, as we find it difficult to see them struggle. But unconditional reassurance only serves as a Band-Aid solution that prevents the child from being in control of their worries. We must try and refrain from being the fixer in these situations, because by learning their own strategies of how to make their worries go away, children will find that their worries shrink and they feel empowered and confident!

## When to Seek Help

For some children worries and fears, whether triggered at home, school, with friends, regarding self-esteem, or sleeping or eating patterns, begin affecting their quality of life. Should you find that your child's well-being is being compromised by their worry, please seek out a local counselling program and refer him or her for further support and guidance.

## How to Use This Booklet

We recommend reading one chapter at time then discussing what you have read with your child. You may wish to read one chapter every couple of days, or even just one a week. There is no rush to complete the activity booklet in one day! Taking your time will give more opportunities to practice the activities and figure out which ones work best for your child.

We also recommend continuing to practice the activities of past days or weeks while adding new activities to the mix. That way, you are building the child's worry toolbox consistently, and using reinforcement.

It's important to understand that every child is different, and that some tools will be more effective than others. Remember that learning any new skill takes practice. It's crucial for these skills to be practiced while the child is emotionally regulated so the tools will become more instinctual when the child is dysregulated. When a child is emotionally regulated, they are able to be in control of their emotions and think constructively about how to cope with feelings.

# Chapter 2

## Co-Regulation Teaches Self-Regulation

"The foundation of self-regulation is that it is only by being regulated that a child develops the ability to self-regulate."

—Dr. Stuart Shanker

One thing to remember is that worries can be positive and purposeful. The end goal is not for children to be worry-free. As helper adults we can assist children in identifying their emotions as well as understanding and managing them in a healthy and effective manner. With this workbook we have a great opportunity to expand your child's emotional vocabulary so they are not simply reliant on the basic emotions of happy, sad, scared, and angry to express and understand themselves.

It's important for you and your child(ren) to get into the habit of noticing and naming feelings. When they cannot, it's our job as helper adults to try and understand what our child is attempting to communicate with their behaviour. Often, we focus solely on trying to "stop" the negative behaviour. By shifting our mindset to trying to decode what our child is communicating, we allow ourselves to see past the negative behaviour and focus on the needs that are driving the behaviour. By addressing our child's underlying needs, research shows that negative behaviours will decrease over time. Our child will feel more understood and therefore less frustrated and potentially angry or alone.

## Co-regulating

As the quote from Dr. Shanker at the beginning of this chapter states, **co-regulating** with your child is critical to helping them regulate big emotions. The process of co-regulation is where a helper adult models a regulated and calm state in order to teach the child healthy management of big emotions.

When we help hold a child's big emotions, we help them feel safe and secure. At times, we may feel that their big emotions are overwhelming, even to us. As challenging as it may be, we must try and remember that if we are emotionally dysregulated (in other words, we do not retain our own composure when our child is worried, afraid, or "acting out"), it adds fuel to the fire and escalates their behaviour.

In the story, Wilbert the Pig did a good job of helping the goats to regulate after their "big scare" by teaching them how to breathe deeply and spend more time in the present moment. Wilbert acted as a great role model for the goats, and indeed all the animals on the farm.

## ACTIVITY
## Lil' Steps for Helper Adults: Notice/Name/Model

**Notice** and begin decoding the needs being communicated in your child's extreme behaviour. What could be underneath the behaviour?

For example, a child at his desk in class who is disrupting the other students might be seen as disrespectful and annoying, when in fact he is feeling embarrassed that he is not able to understand the material.

Then help the child **name** the feeling. Children often do not have the ability to identify or name the emotion they are feeling. Naming it for them helps them build a good vocabulary to express their emotions, and subsequently to be able to manage them. This step of emotional identification is essential to teaching your child how to manage their emotions.

Some simple examples of naming are, "It looks like you are very (insert emotion) right now," or "I see that you are clenching your fists/breathing heavily/stomping your feet/teary. Are you feeling (insert emotion)?"

**Model** healthy ways of coping with emotion—in other words, model emotionally regulated behaviour so that your child can witness it and reproduce it. Doing this (co-regulating) lets your child know that it is okay and safe to feel all emotions, including those big emotions that feel difficult or scary to manage.

For example, be aware of how you are communicating (slow down your speech when you begin to feel angry or annoyed, keep a calm voice and a relaxed body posture).

# Chapter 3

## The Truth about Worry and Fear

**A** **worry** is the result of thinking about things we **fear**. In the story, the goats are great at worrying! Their worries, rather than decreasing when attention is paid to them, continue to grow and grow.

This activity will help your child learn to contain and sit with his or her worries. They will learn that they will have the chance to discuss their worries with you at some point during the day, but for the rest of the time they should try not to worry too much about their fears. Sitting with these big emotions will also teach them that it is okay to feel and manage such difficult emotions.

## ACTIVITY
## Lil' Steps for Everyone: Worried as Worried Can Be . . .
## for 5–10 Minutes a Day!

**Lil' Steps for Children**: Write down a list of things you worry about. Cut them up and put all the worries in the **Goat Worry Box** you have created with your helper adult. When your time in the day comes to talk about your worries, take one worry out of the box at a time and talk about it with your trusted adult. You might not have time to talk about every worry, but that's okay! The **Goat Worry Box** will keep them safe so you can talk about them tomorrow or another day.

**Lil' Steps for Helper Adults**: Together, create a Goat Worry Box. It can be as decorative or as functional as time and materials allow for. Then set aside 5–10 minutes (maximum) a day to focus solely on the worries with your child. You can even set a timer. Once the time is up, put the remaining worries back in the box and "save them" for the next day. If your child brings up his or her worries during the day, encourage them to write them down and put them in the **Goat Worry Box** for your next scheduled worry time.

50

# Chapter 4

## Identifying Worry and Fear in the Body

When we worry or experience fear, our minds like to trick our bodies into thinking we are in danger, even when there is no danger in sight. As mentioned in an earlier chapter, worry and fear have an important function: to keep us safe.

Back in caveperson days, if we had only used our logical (thinking) brain and sometimes not used our instinctual (alarm) brain, we would likely not be here today. Imagine if a caveperson saw a saber-tooth tiger and just thought, "Wow, look at how big his teeth are!" or "I wonder how soft his fur is," they would have very quickly become lunch for the saber-tooth tiger. Instead, the alarm brain needed to kick in, overriding the thinking brain and sending signals to the body to react. The heart would race and send blood to the extremities of the body; the digestive system would shut down to save energy for running or fighting; he or she would even sweat so that if the saber-tooth were to jump on them it might slide right off! We typically refer to this now as the fight, flight or freeze reaction.

The problem, however, is that there are no saber-tooth tigers in our day and age, yet our brains still react as if there are. Being able to understand the signals our bodies are giving us, and what causes us to feel worry and fear, can show us when we are experiencing stress and allow us to put the appropriate coping mechanisms in place.

When it comes to your child, if he or she is able to recognize that they are feeling tension—in their jaw, for instance—they can take a look at what feelings are taking place and try to manage them while the thinking brain is still active. Being aware of how worry affects our bodies as well as our thoughts is key to understanding and taking charge of our worries.

Isn't it interesting that worries can trick both our minds *and* our bodies? Let's begin to understand where your child's worry is tricking their mind and body.

## ACTIVITY
## Lil' Steps for Everyone: Body Awareness and Signs

**Lil' Steps for Helper Adults**: Take steps in your family to normalize the idea that worry likes to trick our minds and bodies. Share with your child where in your body you have felt worry in the past (belly, heart, throat, etc.). By talking openly about something that may be scary or confusing to your child—the strange physical feeling of panic that they might not be able to identify—you are beginning to take some power away from the worry and are providing your child with greater awareness of what these big emotions can do.

Children love hearing that adults have the same emotions they do! It helps normalize these big emotions and make them less scary. Ask your child if they have felt any worry in their bodies today and if so, where they felt it. This will help your child become more aware of his or her body signs and responses, and increase their self-awareness and ability to manage worry or fear before it overcomes them.

**Lil' Steps for Children**: Complete the activity below to learn more about where your body feels worry. Did the goats in the story feel their worry in some of the same places as you?

Where do you feel worry?

# Chapter 5

## The Alarm Responses: Fight, Flight, Freeze

When we feel fear, we respond by **fighting**, **fleeing**, or **freezing**. When children are in their "worry" or "fear brain," it is more difficult for them to understand logical reasoning, such as right and wrong, or provide an answer as to why they are feeling or behaving a certain way. They have difficulty taking in what is being said to them. They need time to regulate and return to their "thinking brain."

As adults we often like to talk, talk, talk. The thing is, when children are in their worry brains, they are not hearing us clearly. And although it may seem like they are not paying attention or even being rude, they may simply not be ready for words at that moment.

### ACTIVITY
### Lil' Steps for Everyone: Fight, Flight, Freeze

**Lil' Steps for Helper Adults:** Using the story, help your child identify the times when Cindy and Cristabelle experienced any or all of the three alarm responses. As they identify them, ask if they can distinguish if the reaction is a **fight, flight,** or **freeze** response. Here is the answer key to assist you.

1) When Cindy or Cristabelle became scared or worried...they fainted! (FREEZE) 2) Cindy was hit with a jolt of energy and she felt like she needed to run. (FLIGHT) 3) Cristabelle's body would freeze; she could feel her feet stuck in the ground. (FREEZE) 4) Cindy jumped straight in the sky, as high as high could be! (FLIGHT) Cristabelle could not move — frozen in her tracks. (FREEZE) 5) They became very angry. "NEVER SNEAK UP ON US LIKE THAT!" Cindy yelled. (FIGHT) 6) They wanted to scream. They wanted to hide. Cristabelle was stuck; as stuck as stuck could be. (FREEZE) Cindy wanted to run, but there was nowhere to go. (FLIGHT) 7) PLOP — the goats both fell to the ground form their big scare. (FREEZE)

**Lil' Steps for Children:** Look through the book with your helper adult and identify the times when Cindy and Cristabelle experience the alarm responses of **fight** (standing up to their fear), **flight** (running away from their fear), or **freeze** (being unable to move because of their fear). Try to name which kind of alarm response happens each time.

# Chapter 6

## As Big as Big Could Be: How to Stop the Worry from Growing

**T**aking time away or distracting ourselves from worrying can be healthy . . . in small doses. The function of distraction is to help move us out of our worry brain and back into our thinking brain. Distraction is not a long-term solution. However, it can be a helpful tool when trying to change a child's mindset, or helping them when they seem stuck in worry. A great form of distraction is *play*! Engaging in a fun activity helps calm your child's emotions.

### ACTIVITY
### Lil' Steps for Everyone: STOP—and Play!

**Lil' Steps for Helper Adults**: When worry takes over, children often forget to have fun! Sit down with your child and create a list of fun things he or she likes to do. Playing, laughing, and being active helps regulate a child's body and mind. Plus, it's fun for us adults to play, too—and children *love it* when we join in! Have fun with your child, and don't be afraid to try new things.

## Activity Booklet

**Lil' Steps for Children**: The more we think about and give into our worries, the less fun we are having. Just think about Cindy and Cristabelle in the story! They worried so much about the coyotes and bears and lions that they forgot about all the fun things they like to do and were missing out on. What are some fun activities you like to do? Draw or write some of your fun activities down with your adult. Then go PLAY!

### Here are a few ideas for fun activities that you can do together!

Play a card or board game

Read your favourite book

Draw or colour

Fly a kite

Go for a walk to the park

Play tag or hide-and-go-seek

Make up a new game together

# Chapter 7

## Showing the Worries Who's Boss!

**N**ow that you have learned about worries and how they like to trick our minds and bodies, let's show them who's boss! When in worry mode we sometimes feel like the worry holds power over us. Now that we know where and why the worries are there, we can take charge and show them that *we* are in control. **They are not the boss of us!**

One great way of doing this is by talking back to the worries. When we notice a worry starting to alarm our body and trick our minds into thinking that something bad is going to happen, we can stand up to the worry and tell it to stop. Encouraging your child to do this will make him or her feel big and strong and make the worry become smaller and smaller.

**Cognitive distortions** are "brain tricks" caused by fear and worry. You may find that children who worry also struggle with such thought distortions as: **all-or-nothing thinking** ("My day was horrible!" or "My day was perfect!"); **emotional reasoning** ("If I'm feeling this way then it must be true," or "If I'm feeling bad then it must be bad"); **catastrophic thinking** (obsessing over irrational worst-case scenarios); **over-generalizing** (making assumptions based on a single event—"It was scary last time so it will be scary this time"); and **magnification** (making a big deal out of something small—"My friend didn't say hello to me so they must not like me anymore").

We all have a habit sometimes of thinking in these distorted ways. The important thing is to be very clear that these ways of thinking are simply products of feelings of fear and worry, rather than actual facts.

## ACTIVITY
## Lil' Steps for Everyone: Putting Cognitive Distortions in Their Place

**Lil' Steps for Helper Adults:** Read the story with your child and identify times when Cindy and Cristabelle experience cognitive distortions (brain tricks) and what kind each one might be. Here is the answer key to assist you.

Page 6 and 7: Catastrophizing. Cindy's what ifs. Page 10: Overgeneralizing. Cindy assumed that the coyotes, bears, and lions were coming back based on one occasion where the coyote had visited the farm. Page 16: All-or-nothing thinking. When the pig asked the goats to come out and watch for shooting stars, the goats answered, "Oh no, no, no, we can NEVER stay out at night when ALL of the scary things come out". Page 18: Magnification. When the goats hear a branch snap, they immediately assumed that it must be a bear or coyote or a lion ready to pounce. But it was in fact just a branch.

Get your child to identify 3 tricks that their brain does when they worry.

**Lil' Steps for Children:** Once you have discussed with your adult some of the brain tricks Cindy and Cristabelle struggle with in the story, think about some things you can tell your worries when your brain is trying to trick your mind and body into being afraid.

If you feel stuck, or aren't sure, here are some things you can tell them! (Try to come up with some more yourself!)

# GO AWAY!
# I KNOW WHAT YOU ARE TRYING TO DO, AND I WON'T LET YOU!
# YOU ARE NOT TRICKING ME TODAY!
# I WILL NOT LET YOU TAKE AWAY MY FUN!
# I AM THE BOSS, NOT YOU!

# Chapter 8

## "Piggy Belly Breathing"

**N**ow that they have talked back to their worries and showed them who is boss, let's work on helping your child bring their body back toward calm. Breathing is a great way to bring our bodies back to a place of calm. I know it may sound silly, and you might be thinking, "Well, I breathe all the time! How will breathing help?" But by doing deep "piggy belly breathing" you and your child are becoming more aware of your breathing, which helps to calm your body and mind.

So, how do you do deep piggy belly breathing like Wilbert does? First, you must take a in a BIG, deep breath, so that the air doesn't just reach your lungs but *also* your belly. Then, when the air has reached your belly, hold it for a second and then SLOOOWWWLLLYYY let it out. As you do this exercise you should see your belly going up and down.

## ACTIVITY
## Lil' Steps for Everyone: Piggy Belly Bubble Breathing

**Lil' Steps for Helper Adults:** Show your child how to do the piggy belly breathing using the description in the paragraph above. Once they have the hang of it, bring bubbles into the equation! You can either buy a container of bubble mix or make it yourself with dish soap. Make sure your child is focusing on the **deep inhale** and the **slow exhale,** and on the **rise and fall of their belly** while they breathe.

It is helpful to count to **4** when breathing in; then hold for **1**; then count to **4** while breathing out and finally, hold for another **1.** Continue this process until the child is feeling calmer.

The in-and-out breathing helps regulate his or her breathing, calms down their body responses, and brings them back to their logical or thinking brain. The bubbles also provide them with a happy visual, and the goal of blowing the biggest bubble or as many bubbles as possible keeps them focused on a slow exhale.

**Lil' Steps for Children:** Take a deep breath in, then slooooowly blow it out, trying to make as many piggy bubbles as you can! Make sure that your breath reaches allll the way to your belly! See what happens to your breathing and body worries when you practise piggy bubble breathing! Soon you will be breathing calmly, just like Wilbert the Pig.

# Chapter 9

## the Joy Jar

The Joy Jar is a tool that helps children focus and be mindful. This activity also asks them to *visualize* (imagine) their favourite place, which helps them to create a state of calm and a feeling of safety. You can encourage your child to do piggy belly breathing at the same time.

The Joy Jar is a physical representation of what's going on in your child's mind and body when they feel worried or afraid. Making the ideas and lessons concrete helps your child to "see" the problem, which makes it easier to address.

### ACTIVITY
### Lil' Steps for Everyone: As Calm as Calm Can Be

**Lil' Steps for Helper Adults**: Help your child write down or draw their favourite place to be. To help them, ask them if they could be anywhere, doing anything in the whole wide world, where would they be, and what would they be doing? Who would be there?

Once the exercise is complete, it's time to create the Joy Jar. Explain to your child that the water represents calmness and is the first thing to add. Note that warm water works best for the Joy Jar. The second ingredient is the glitter glue, which represents their worries. Help the child tighten the lid of the jar and then tell them to shake the jar as hard as they can. Ask them what they see. The glitter glue will be stuck together. Explain to them, "This is how our worries stay if we don't learn how to manage them. Our worries can feel stuck like the glue, or feel heavy in our minds."

Next, add the loose glitter. This represents their favourite place! The glitter is beautiful and bright. The final step is the clear gel tacky glue. This represents the work your child is currently doing: learning about their worries, taking charge of them, and becoming more confident and in control. This last ingredient is the key ingredient to making the Joy Jar! The clear gel tacky glue will separate all the glitter and create a beautiful swirl of sparkles (their favourite place) and water (calm). When the clear gel tacky glue breaks up the glitter glue, this allows the worries to go away and become their favourite place.

Encourage your child to breathe their piggy belly breaths and imagine that they are in their special place as they watch the sparkles float to the bottom of the jar. You can now explain to your child that they can be happy, calm, and joyful, even when they have worries (the glitter glue) included in their Joy Jar!

64

# Activity Booklet

**Lil' Steps for Children**: Write down or draw your favourite place to be with your adult. Then it's time to create your Joy Jar together!

Now you have your Joy Jar, whenever you feel worries coming back into your mind or body, you can shake, shake, shake your Joy Jar and think about your special place! As the sparkles fall to the bottom, take some deep piggy belly breaths and imagine yourself doing your favourite activity, with your favourite people, at your favourite place ever! And remember that just like the ingredients in the Joy Jar, you can still feel calm and be happy even when you have worries. I hope this helps you feel as calm as calm can be!

65

# Chapter 10

## Sitting Like a Pig in Mud

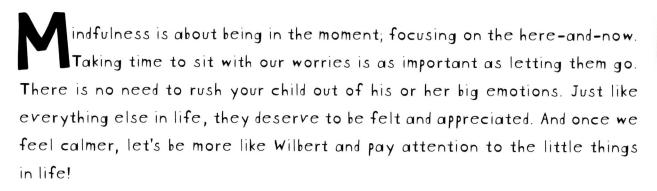

**M**indfulness is about being in the moment; focusing on the here-and-now. Taking time to sit with our worries is as important as letting them go. There is no need to rush your child out of his or her big emotions. Just like everything else in life, they deserve to be felt and appreciated. And once we feel calmer, let's be more like Wilbert and pay attention to the little things in life!

This activity teaches the helper adults that they also must learn to be okay and comfortable with sitting with big emotions (theirs and their child's). By providing a safe space for children to express their big emotions, and responding in an understanding and non-judgmental manner, you will provide comfort for your child while they are sitting in the mud. In this way they will start to realize that their worries are not as scary as they thought.

As parents and caregivers, we understand that sitting with big emotions is sometimes challenging and difficult and we may find ourselves becoming dysregulated along with the child. The more we pay attention to and become aware of our own self-regulation, the better we can co-regulate with our child.

## Activity
## Lil' Steps for Everyone: Sitting in the Mud

**Lil' Steps for the Helper Adult:** A great way to be mindful is to use your senses. Using some putty or mud, play with the material, and with your child, explore it using your senses of touch, smell, sight, and hearing. Ask your child to tell you how it feels, how it looks, how it smells, and how it sounds. Let them play with the putty and make something from it. Encourage him or her to explain what they are creating as they are playing.

Expand this exercise in mindfulness by taking a walk outside and asking your child to use his or her senses as a guide. What do they see, hear, smell, touch, and taste? This teaches your child to notice and become more aware of their surroundings, and in turn become more present, and increasingly, more happy.

**Lil' Steps for Children:** Play with the putty and answer your helper adult's questions about your senses. Does it change once you've played with it for a while? Do you like how it smells? What does it feel like when you stretch it slowly or pull it apart quickly? What do you see the putty do when it stretches? How does it feel when you stretch it slowly and wrap it around your fingers?

# Chapter 11

## It All Comes Down to Healthy Relationships

"There are two lasting bequests we can give our children:
One is roots. The other is wings."

—Hodding Carter Jr.

In the end, healthy brain activity and a happy lifestyle is all about relationships. Enjoy your child. Learn as much as you can about their strengths, likes, and dislikes. Be curious about them while accepting them for who they are and what they bring to your relationship and your family. One of the best gifts we can give a child is to get to know them wholeheartedly—that is, freely and without expectations. By providing a caring, safe, and judgment-free environment, you will allow your child to explore, be vulnerable, share, and become their best self, while also mitigating the feelings of shame, guilt, **weakness**, and self-blame that are often the cause of big emotions like worry and fear. A child will become who they are believed to be: if we see the child from a strength-based perspective, the child is allowed to gain confidence in who they are and will become.

You are providing a physical, emotional, and psychological connection every time you spend time with your child, whether it's by going through these activities, creating new ones, or simply being present together.

The ability to be aware of and understand fear and worry will normalize these emotions and allow them to become more manageable.

COMING SOON! Book two of the Lil' Steps Farm Series!

If you loved our wonderful farm animals, you can purchase our tool kit and other sensory tools at our online shop: www.lilstepswellnessfarm.net.

ISBN
978-1-5255-2552-0 (Hardcover)
978-1-5255-2553-7 (Paperback)
978-1-5255-2554-4 (eBook)

*1. EDUCATION, COUNSELING*

Printed in Canada

# About the Author

LUCY SLOAN is a counsellor and the owner of Lil Steps Miniatures & Wellness Farm in St. Malo, Manitoba. After a terrible head injury turned her life upside down, Lucy learned firsthand the debilitating effects of anxiety. Two miniature horses proved crucial to her recovery, and from this experience the dream of Lil Steps Farm was born. She has been providing children and teens with animal-assisted counselling ever since.

"Each animal on the farm has a story to tell. I wanted to share their stories with other children with the hope of helping them to learn about mental health challenges and how to overcome them," says Lucy.

Lucy lives with her family and her animal co-workers at Lil' Steps Farm, where together they play, explore nature, and enjoy being in the moment together.

JOANNE LARIVIERE is a mental health counsellor for children and youth and has held various positions in the counselling field for the past 12 years. Her passion for working with children developed from her personal struggle with anxiety at a young age and wishing there would have been more supports available to her. Joanne believes that early intervention and education are key in helping children and youth who are experiencing mental health struggles.

Joanne lives in St-Malo with her three children and enjoys spending time exploring and playing with them. She loves to garden, read, cycle, and go for walks in her spare time. Becoming a mom has been one of Joanne's greatest joys!